A Puddle of Words

Poems of the Human Condition

BY

April Seymour

This book is dedicated to anyone who has ever been stirred by human emotion or experience.

Thank you to my loved ones for your invaluable support.

Special thanks to my daughter, Peyton, for your feedback and encouragement. You've grown into an amazing young woman, and I'm incredibly proud of you.

Content Guidance: This book contains references to sensitive subjects, such as violence and self-harm.

Contents

You Pass Me Over

I see your eyes scan the room,
and you pass me over.

Last year, last month, last week,
because I was silent, you thought I was meek.

You find the most beautiful one in the room.
This wouldn't be me, or so you assume.

You walk like perhaps you have something to prove.
You think the whole world is watching you move.

Your choice has been made, and so you sit down.
But soon after sitting, your face meets a frown.

The beautiful one is too dull for you.
You wanted the beauty with some substance too.

You stand and your eyes scan the room,
and you pass me over.

For now, for later, forever,
because I was silent, I wasn't too clever.

You choose your next victim based on the green.
The well isn't dry if you know what I mean.

You're positive this time you're finished selecting.
Attractive and loaded, like you were expecting.

But soon you discover the rich one's too cruel,
and after a while you move from your stool.

You notice someone you hadn't before,
but you have to move quick; I'm nearing the door.

You reach me and put your hand on my shoulder.
I'm scarcely impressed, so I pass you over.

In the Dark

To be together is forbidden.
Pain for them, but forgiven.
Now alone, much apart.
All the pressure on my heart.
So, you ask to be with me, to have me once again.
Longing to go back to it, to how we once had been.
You missed it, so did I.
Didn't expect us to cry.
Always knew it wouldn't last.
In the dark we're in the past.

<u>A Collection of Stars</u>

You said you remembered me
in your collection of stars.
I was one of the brightest,
yet your imagery mars.

Our memories were vivid,
but you made them dimmer.
I sparkled in darkness,
and you saw me shimmer.

Like a lone firefly,
I was but one star.
Gather me. Collect me.
Put me in a jar.

Love is Blind

On the phone, in the bed,
looking in your eyes.
I couldn't see if it was truth,
or if it was just lies.

Counting precious moments,
as if they were our last.
How unaware of this I was,
'til present became past.

And I remember still,
I could not let it go.
I would ask, "do you love me yet?"
"I'm not sure, but I think so."

If I Only Knew

So, I suppose you're touching her again,
and more than now and then.
Your hands. Those hands that used to touch me.
Those arms that used to hold me. Now her property.
Well, what can I say? We're back where we started.
You left me broken-hearted.
And if I only knew,
I never would've fell for you.
I was unaware
of what was there.
Blinded by your lies,
your falsehood fooled my eyes.
Since my eyes deceived me,
I'm watching so intently.
Unable to trust,
unable to love.
You killed that precious part
of my unsuspecting heart.
I will never forgive you for what you've done.
Killing my strength where it had begun.
You created animosity,
the anger deep inside of me.
And if I only knew,
I never would've fell for you.

I Still Remember

I still remember how things were breaking down.
I still remember your face holding a frown.
I know we fought and were not getting along,
and I know I did so many damned things wrong.

But I didn't know that you'd leave the top off.
Half of me was with you. Now I'm partly lost.
What I have left is nothing but some baggage.
Pain that I don't need. Here, why don't you take this?

I still remember that day on the phone.
At the kitchen table, I sat all alone.
I tried to cling to each ounce of what we had.
I still remember being helplessly sad.

Dumping out emotions I had stored away.
Gradually built up for that special day.
I still remember that you were such a fake.
Giving those lies you had. Every lie I'd take.

Carrying the torment you brought upon me,
I hope you grasp it someday. Maybe you'll see.
I still remember how much I once loved you.
and I'm sickened that the truth is I still do.

<u>Overboard</u>

The knot in my stomach is tightening its grip.
At this point I feel like abandoning ship.
I'm sick of the worries; the waves of the past.
I never can tell if the present will last.
I just want to sail this sea to the future.
The knot doesn't seem to get any looser.
What would the captain do if I said,
"Man overboard," and then I was dead?

Foolish Flowers

A garden full of flowers, blossoming with life.
Too innocent to realize pollination's rife.

The wind blowing him about; typical circumstances.
Creating a certain mood for the bud he entrances.

He, being the insect, the flying honey bee,
that sucks out the nectar and drains them selfishly.

Once he's fully nourished, the ego that he feeds
carries him on breezes to propagate more seeds.

High on nature's sweet candy, he is stalking here and
there.
The yielding foolish flowers still remaining unaware.

The blossoms in the garden, dwelling in the rain,
are wet with condemnation and stricken with pain.

Tornado in a Small Town

Take a look at you. Tell me who you see.
Is the reflection you stare into what you'd like to be?
Are you yourself, satisfactorily?
Look just once more. Who do you see?
Is the image looking back a picture of the truth?
Or is it just society prodding at your youth?
Is it all your friends that you must try to be?
Is it just your parents' pressures that you see?
Are you trapped inside yourself, waiting to come out?
A tornado in a small town, a flood inside a drought?
Candy coated pain, soft inside a shell?
Sugar-sprinkled outside to cover up your hell?
Are you a gift-wrapped package, underneath the tree,
covering up the fragile parts that only you can see?

Wasteland

It's just a waste of time.
We do it anyway.

We do the common things we do,
We do them every day.

Everything is done in excess,
yet nothing's getting done.

And everyone is still smiling,
yet no one's having fun.

It's a stirring reality
that no one wants to face.

So, rather than slowing it down,
we just pick up the pace.

It is just a wired wasteland.
No human connection.

Lacking moral values.
Devoid of protection.

Insignificant

When you stop and watch the world from afar
you feel how insignificant you are.

<u>Awareness</u>

The rage is clear, no longer here.
The hate, the chains, have disappeared.
I've found the key; let freedom ring.
We take for granted such a thing.
Believe. Become what you can now,
because it could be gone somehow.
And don't let blind eyes be your guide,
because you can't see things that hide.
You'll never know when reality is about,
and then you're shocked when it comes out.
Things are never what they seem,
and life is never like a dream.
Just be careful when you blink.
You're missing more than you may think.

The Rebound

He said I am a butterfly,
and he is my cocoon.
That I will fly away from him,
and it will end too soon.
He said he is a lily pad,
and I will jump away.
As if he were a resting point
on just another day.
He thinks he is a stopping place
for me to heal my heart,
and I will leave him here alone,
behind, and torn apart.
He thinks he is a rebound stage,
any means to an end.
Threading the needle, stitching up,
so I can simply mend.
Maybe I've been distant.
Not sure why he's feeling this way.
Perhaps if I work harder,
I can prove him wrong someday.

Blue-Green Eyes

Blue-green eyes stare into mine.
As each our tattered hearts combine.
You hold me close and give me love.
You ask me what I'm thinking of.
Such a strong and thoughtful man.
You tell me how beautiful I am.
And even if I disagree,
You will reassure for me.
You tell me that you hate to go.
I'm thankful that you love me so.
I'd like to share with you a home,
hold you, keep you as my own.

Why I Love You

I love the way you hold me,
your arms that wrap so tight.
Cradling arms that keep me dreaming
long throughout the night.

I love the way you kiss me,
your lips so warm and sweet.
So sensuous it's not hard
for my heart to skip a beat.

I love the way you want me
when we are all alone,
and I can feel your closeness
as stiffly as it is grown.

I love the way you show me
how much you love me so.
Your hands appearing around my waist
quickly as they're thrown.

I love the way you touch me,
those certain things you do,
when you come up behind me
and I know it must be you.

I love how you make me laugh,
the way you make me smile,
if I'm hurt or I'm upset,
or just with you for a while.

I love that you still want to
make our shared future last,
when we had struggled terribly
to make it through the past.

I love the way you love me,
in all the things you do,
and these are just some reasons why
I am in love with you.

The Lover's Night

No matter what elements will be,
we will still have you and me.
In the blistering heat of winter
and the deadness of spring,
you will be my shelter
and I'll be your everything.
When summer's fall and autumn leaves,
we will not be one that grieves.
When falling rain is dry like fire
and all the silence does conspire,
we may still laugh on downcast days.
We shall not part on joining ways.
In the darkest dawn we'll be all right,
for we will have the lover's night.

<u>Drifting</u>

It seems as though lately
my feelings won't come out right.
I sit and search for perfect words
long throughout the night.
It seems as though I'm constantly
searching to express
my particular uncertainties,
my constant loneliness.
I'm so afraid of losing you,
though you say I'm not.
When you say you love me,
it truly means a lot.
Then it changes and you seem
far away from me.
It hurts me when you pull away.
If only you could see.
I wish that you would reach out
and hold me close to you.
I see that you are drifting
and there's nothing I can do.

Holding On

Holding up my head,
I hold on to my heart.
Trying to hold myself together
since we've been apart.

Looking around to see you.
Somehow, I see you there.
You vanish then before me.
I blink, you disappear.

Oh love, what are we doing?
Trying to pretend?
Don't you see it? It's clear to me.
This time is causing end.

Our love is slowly fading,
and soon we'll grow apart.
Soon I'll be a stranger to
your once familiar heart.

Am I the only one
that cries these helpless tears?
Sweetness, is it only me
that clings on to those years?

I Let it Go

As trite as the night, your mood is like coffee.
So bittersweet, I drink the flow.

As soft as a cloud, your love is like air.
Unable to grasp, I let it go.

As bright as the sun, your truth is like fire.
Burning my eyes, I start to cry.

As mute as a rose, your voice is like thorns.
Piercing my heart, you say goodbye.

Trauma

I was just a kid when the woman ran out.
I heard her blood curdling shrieks. I heard her shout.

She ran to the front while sobbing and screaming.
"My baby! My baby!" The child wasn't breathing.

Alarm running through me when hearing the sounds
of petrified shocks throwing life out of bounds.

The disturbing scene battered with shock and pause.
Her boyfriend was there. It wasn't a natural cause.

She wailed in distress at the top of her voice.
Her baby was dead. She was given no choice.

Decades recalling despairing words she cried,
witness to her trauma, I remain horrified.

Where Death Begins

The darkness shrouds her like a cloak.
She nearly suffocates; she chokes.
Her air is pinched. Her throat is closed.
Her mind is stiff. Her heart is posed.
He waits for breath; he waits for blood.
Her lungs are thick, like filled with mud.
The pain it crushes her. A vise.
She explodes, ignoring advice.
Her bones, they cry. Her body aches.
Her world is shattered. Her earth quakes.
Immobilized as she chagrins,
he ends her life where death begins.

The Man with Soiled Hands

When you are in the ground
so cold you do not shiver,
I hope your box of death
gives you a moldy sliver.

I hope you writhe in hell,
with Satan burning your soul.
I pray he rips your heart out
and leaves you with a hole.

Smothering you forever,
without a breath of air,
I will stand by and snicker,
and love that I don't care.

You are less than slime
inside a nasty septic drain.
You only deeply deserve
to be riddled with pain.

Inconceivably, you're showing
no apparent qualms
with deplorability
or having filthy palms.

You are the lowest form on earth.
The vilest that stands.
You've done such disgraceful things.
You sleep with soiled hands.

Autumn's Child

In the deepest crimson shades of red
upon the autumn trees,
falling blood growing cold and thick,
chilled, dripping from veins of leaves.

Prodigiously colored things
uncontrolled and dying away.
Her beauty is illusory,
the deception of decay.

Autumn's lovely child is
dark and mysterious.
Creative, artistic.
Loving, masochistic.

Self-destructive and self-defeating.
Summer's scorched heart barely beating.
The blazing fire has now succumbed
to the knowledge of what is to come.

Alive with passion in the sun,
although autumn soon forgets
the warmth experienced in that time
and what its love begets.

She's fallen. What remains is memory
of something once grasped.
Drifting into the wind,
autumn's loss is so painful and vast.

Still Waters

In a calm and quiet site.
Something's blowing, gaining might.
Finding force, it plays to win.
Slowly growing, rushing in.
Once still waters under storm,
now arisen; taken form.
Lightning flashes, shouts thunder.
Faultless lives cast asunder.
Death now reaches what was born.
Silence listens as they mourn.

When I Needed You

Not last night, but the night before,
you showed up knocking at my door.
Not expecting this to occur,
I was glad still; of this, I'm sure.
I am quite thankful you were there,
although I gave you quite a scare.
Some things are just beyond control.
I guess my past had taken toll.
To stop this part of me, I tried,
but I shed tears I could not hide.
You showed me that you care that night.
You cried with me and held me tight.
I was scared you would turn away,
and not return another day.
Giving me more than I can tell,
you called to make sure I was well.
Thank you for knowing what to do,
being there when I needed you.

By the Light of the Moon

Naked, he
is next to me.
In bed,
asleep,
deliriously.
In my blood,
he is my love.
My life,
my dreams,
my world, thereof.

<u>As You Sleep</u>

You snore sometimes. I don't mind.
We're tangled up together.
I revel in your arm over me, around me.
Your caressing hands.
Our legs and feet wrapped.
Your skin. Your chest hair. My hand running through it.
You breathe me in, pull me closer,
kiss my shoulder.
It's tactile. Tangible.
Laying beside you, feeling your warmth,
I give myself permission,
to feel loved.
To be happy.

Regret

When I met you, I was wounded
from someone else's lies.
I didn't trust your words.
I couldn't believe your eyes.
I kept myself shielded
and I held back my heart.
I wanted to be what you needed.
Instead I tore us apart.

<u>Eggshells</u>

There are eggshells on the floor,
and I cannot get to the door.

The phone won't ring,
it's off the hook,
and my best friend
is now a book.

I cannot breathe.
(No oxygen in here!)
I cannot see.
(The air's not clear.)

There are eggshells on the floor,
and I cannot get to the door.

Three Things

Sometimes I just wonder
how this came to be.
I remember when at first,
I thought you cared for me.

Foolishly, I fell for you
but kept it in disguise.
I'm not quite sure just what it was.
Possibly your eyes?

Maybe certain things you said
or things you did for me.
Maybe it was none of those.
Perhaps it was all three.

Interesting that all this pain
is what I tried to avoid.
It feels you're playing games with me,
and I guess that I'm annoyed.

I'm not surprised though, you're a man,
and I've gotten used to those.
Maybe they just like to hurt me.
I'm a target, I suppose.

Off my guard, I hadn't prepared
myself enough for this.
Stupidly, I found some comfort
in your loving kiss.

Didn't realize that I'd be
simply tossed away,
and I just hope tomorrow
I feel better than today.

Resentment

I felt happiness, and sadly, it brought me pain.
A reminder of the loss I had to gain.
Unable to grasp it, the wish slipped through my hands.
What could I have done to appease your demands?
We cannot be fulfilled. There is no contentment.
I lay in my bed and suck up resentment.
A short-lived success, losing before it started.
Did both of us know before we departed?

<u>Unrequited</u>

Just another day like any other
and you saw me so plain and shapeless
as if I was your brother.

I walked beside you in the position I assume
and the only thing that I could do
was smell your damned perfume.

I try not to look at your face much anymore.
It tells me what I cannot have.
What do I need that reminder for?

It hurts too much to see your eyes.
So I listen to your voice
as a useless compromise.

I Needed More

I didn't plan the fallout
of this unfortunate thing.
And by ignoring all doubt
what sad mayhem it did bring.
I needed much more from you
than you were willing to give.
But perhaps you always knew
it was how you couldn't live.
I know I asked for too much.
For that, you resented me.
We were out of hope and touch
in more ways than I could see.

Disappointed

I thought more of you.
I respected you.
I thought I had a fair idea of who you are.

You seemed smart.
You appeared kind to me.
Maybe I wished you were more than I saw from afar.

It was my mistake,
and I was left in the wake
of a miscommunication I now see.

With spirit broken,
my eyes are open.
I know now, it's less about you and more about me.

<u>Ivory Tower</u>

In the ivory tower, you're always looking down.
High above the others. Keep polishing your crown.

A burden it must be, with silver on your tongue.
The taste of persuasion and privilege to be young.

Glass House

She lives in a glass house
and still she threw stones.
Ripping, tearing at your flesh
until she reached your bones.
Lies and fabrications.
She tried to make a wedge.
Pushing you and trying you
until you reached the edge.
Even when you thought
you'd put her in her place,
she denied the accusations
and lied right to your face.

Conspicuous Behavior

You, with your insensate demeanor.
You, with your blank stare.
You're totally unfeeling,
and utterly unaware.
You, with your insidious plan,
your disloyal conspiracy.
You are oblivious
to what I can see.
You, with your fulsome love,
your unctuous compliments.
You are so blind to
the clarity it presents.
You, with your façade.
Your impenetrable eyes.
You didn't know
I could hear right through your lies.

<u>Excuses</u>

You always send mixed signals.
I think that you are torn.
Conflicted between what you feel
and actions you've worn.

You say things in anger
and then try to take them back.
You know you can't make up
for the self-control you lack.

I've felt so fucking lonely.
You never seem to care.
But you, by far, must be
the loneliest person anywhere.

You can make excuses,
blame others for what you do,
but the fact of the matter is,
you're only fucked up because of you.

Sugar Plums

I'd like to sleep with sugar plums dancing in my head.
Rather, I have nightmares plaguing my slumber instead.

Originally, I thought,
this page had long been turned.
I find that I was wrong,
and the book should have been burned.

Trapped in chapters of my life repeating in my mind.
Where is the peace and solitude I am yet to find?

Waking up in tears again after I fall asleep.
Calling for a contentment I cannot seem to keep.

The past comes back to haunt me
and will not let me go.
Maybe it was buried beneath
the cold, winter snow.

Now that it has melted, it reminds me of back then.
How to get the past behind? When can I sleep again?

Crying My Words

I cannot say it out loud
because my words become tears.
They're dropping out like puddles
that were waiting in arrears.
I am fighting; I'm grappling
with how to articulate
feelings going unexpressed.
Things I cannot consummate.

Damaged

I'm convinced she's evil, pathological, psychotic.
Nobody can heal her, not a saint or a neurotic.

<u>Diamond</u>

I watched you for a while,
and kept my feelings from you.
Then you opened up to me
and said you felt it too.

Confessed you felt it first.
When I never thought you could.
True, you fell in love with me.
I never thought you would.

You opened up your heart
and put something in my hand.
I had so many questions,
but now I understand.

You gave me a rare gift,
shining bright for me to see.
Your love so very precious.
The diamond you gave me.

The Music

Filling the air, our music swelled
with tides of ebb and flow.
Magical notes, they played for us,
rising high and falling low.

But when the orchestra dwindled,
told diminuendo,
we danced no more, you left me, and
I cried with crescendo.

Remaining Pain

It is a mystery to me,
what exactly your eyes do see.
I'm unsure over lots of things,
and frightened over what life brings.
Pain of my mind still lives inside.
This thing I sometimes try to hide.
The gods they know what really be.
The anguish deep inside of me.
I ask you to take care of you,
the thing for me I cannot do.

<u>Naïve</u>

You never made a sacrifice for this heart.
You were totally selfish from the start.
Too consumed with your own burning needs
to give a second thought to me.

Didn't expect me to get under your skin,
but I did, and you're always needing in.
You say you miss me and you want me.
But do you think you can love me?

I know my naivete was juvenile,
and I will no longer walk in denial.

I know now when you ask me to spend the night
your intention is not to inflict plight.
Your question is simply meant to be
as uncomplicated as it seems.

It's merely your longing controlling you.
You're not impervious to what I do.
Desire for what I do so well
is something that you cannot quell.

I know my naivete was juvenile,
and I will no longer walk in denial.

<u>Your Greatest Vice</u>

You loved me once. You loved me twice.
Your greatest sin; your greatest vice.
Don't love me anymore, you say?
I'm sure you will again someday.

Die Away

Carelessly,
I take a breath,
every minute
nearing death.

Think about it,
every day,
each of us,
we die away.

Now isn't that
a scary thought?
To think that death
is what life brought.

Once alive,
we begin to die.
Cannot stop it
if we try.

How pointless it is,
to live one day,
when we will just
die anyway.

He

He comes and goes like a breeze,
brushing my memories.
Sometimes he is real,
sometimes just a dream.
Will he stay or go?
I wait to know.
It's like he's a fantasy,
always tempting me.
Should I give in, and be completely vulnerable?
Should I let go? Is it even possible?
He shows me what love is.
I'm not so used to this.
He's nothing I've seen before.
He always wants to give me more.
He nourishes me any way he can.
He isn't just a wonderful man.
He is the light in my darkest hours.
He gives back happiness my sadness devours.
He is a blessing to my soul.
He makes my broken heart feel whole.
Slowly now, I will allow myself to completely let go.
And he will own my every breath and he is all I'll
know.
I think it's possible, and I believe
that he is all the love I need.

Ubiquitous You

Ubiquitous you, never rue
that you are you, keeping true.
Inside, behind, and close next to,
you stay with me. You always do.

I smell you on the pillow.
I feel you in the air.
Even while you're gone from me,
you still are everywhere.

Frequently our talks
begin evoking thought.
You're present in me
like happiness we've sought.

Ubiquitous you, never rue
that you are you, keeping true.
Inside, behind, and close next to,
you stay with me. You always do.

Love notes left behind,
I hold them very dear.
With you in my heart,
know you are always here.

Miles away we had our love.
You were with me in song.
Far apart yet still entwined,
we weren't kept down for long.

Ubiquitous you, never rue
that you are you, keeping true.
Inside, behind, and close next to,
you stay with me. You always do.

To My Love

United mind and body,
united in the soul,
you have filled an empty space,
and now my heart is whole.
I no longer have to wander
alone and with defeat,
for you have given so much love
and made my life complete.
You emanate with beauty,
with strength, and so much more.
It's all these things about you
I honor and adore.

I Waited for You

I looked at you through rose-colored glasses.
For years, you were impeccable.
Undefeated. Invincible.

I waited for you.

No one, anywhere, could compare to you.
Past, present, future, forever.
In my dreams, always together.

I waited for you.

You stood with my day, watching from afar.
Wrapped around me, I felt your arms.
You waited for me, kept me warm.

I waited for you.

Time passed; finally, you stood before me.
I looked at you and saw difference.
An unimagined imminence.

Heartbreakingly, I discovered what's true.
Proof you wanted something new, and
held her while I waited for you.

Up All Night

My eyes are growing weary from the sleep I've lost.
Up all night deciding how I can pay the cost.

Trying not to worry. I no longer have you.
Avoidance isn't working. Don't know what to do.

Tell me how to do it, how to become strong.
How do I pass time, so this is not so long?

When does all the hurting stop? Will it go away?
Sometimes I don't think it will and it's here to stay.

Don't you know I need you? That you are all I need?
Deep inside me, locked away, how my heart does bleed.

Yearning for your love, can't stand to be like this.
Wanting you to hold me, dying for a kiss.

Music in the air, a melody in my head.
Echoing a nightmare that haunts me in my bed.

I cannot do without you. No, I can't go on.
Someone has to help me. Oh no, what have I done?

Time to go to sleep now. Time to take a rest.
Up all night just crying. Wish me all the best.

Skin

I am standing in the dark, naked,
with my skin peeled back.

The room nearly black and still,
almost silent, but not quite.
If I scream, will you soothe me,
or put me out with the light?

I am standing in the dark, naked,
with my skin peeled back.

The blood sits idle on me,
like a soft-covered blanket of dough.
Not running, not spoiling, just waiting.
Why wait? I don't know.

I am standing in the dark, naked,
with my skin peeled back.

Yet, I can see your eyes.
The color never goes away.
I can smell the air, your cologne,
like it was yesterday.

I am standing in the dark, naked,
with my skin peeled back.

One of us is a victim,
a gentle lamb with a blade.
I'll see if you bleed like me.
Now look what a mess you made.

I am crying in the dark, naked,
with my skin peeled back.

<u>In These Times</u>

All those years of anger.
All those years of pain.
I held in my tears,
hardly staying sane.
Too much time with heartbreaks,
losses big and small.
No one cares to listen.
No one cares at all.
Now the times are different.
In these times I cry.
I let out my anger and
don't even have to try.
Pain comes just as often though.
That much is still true.
But now I'm not alone.
I've hurt others too.

<u>Empty Tunnel</u>

Darkness in the tunnel, demons all around.
Walking with the spirits, deep beneath the ground.
Hide the ache inside, no tears to be shed.
Anger in the mind, no blood to be bled.
Hatred and frustration, without emotional time.
Shredded hopes for love, life an endless rhyme.
Happiness the cover, hold inside the pain.
Driven by the terror, slowly gone insane.
Succumb to deadly medicine; but I will not weep.
Close these eyes and shudder, then lay down to sleep.

Nothing Else to Give

To feed your stomach, growling strong.
You have been hungry for so long.
As I'm consumed by caustic fears,
you may consume my burning tears,
trickling and pouring from my eyes.
I hide behind this forged disguise.
Lick my blackened, salty water.
I would give these to no other.

Take away this agony.
Become every part of me.
I have nothing else to give.
Will you take these while I live?
Even if my soul is poor,
and I cannot give one more,
you may eat my withered skin.
Nourish you; so frail and thin.

A Sequel

Darkness. Silence. A moonlit night.
Empty morning. Sun shining bright.
Crying. Stabbing. Attempted suicide.
Waking. Aching. Lucky no one died.
Fortunate? I say not, for it was my attempt.
Escaping from the anguish, this is what I dreamt.
A second blood loss, this is what I'll try.
A sequel, successful, this time I will die.

<u>Broken</u>

One day she slipped down through my hands
and fell right to the floor.
Suddenly, I couldn't recognize
who she was anymore.

She shattered into pieces
I couldn't glue together,
and I began to wonder if
she'd be like that forever.

I tried to grasp the fragments
of her broken shell,
but all it did was cut up
my hands to bloody hell.

I saw the remnants of what once was,
but now had gone away.
I tried to make her whole,
but there was nothing I could say.

One day I saw the mirror,
and all that I could see,
was a stranger in my view.
She didn't look like me.

I left myself in a pile,
helplessly lying there.
It got so bad with time,
I didn't even care.

Torn up hands and all,
I finally grabbed what I could.
I didn't know how to fix her,
but I knew somehow, I would.

I taped up the cracks
and put her together.
I thought my accomplishment
was pretty clever.

I expected her to be
like she had been before,
but with all those scars on her,
she's not the same girl anymore.

Running

Together we trudge, through sordid decay.
Frantically running, to slip away.

Unanticipated

She looks at me like she is glaring.
She doesn't like to catch me staring.
I look at her with adoration.
So wrapped up in our deviation.
She'll catch me looking and roll her eyes.
Her presentation sometimes disguise.
Those that know her are fascinated.
A blessing unanticipated.
So happy to have her in their space,
and see her beautiful, smiling face.
They feel just as elated as me.
But they don't know the intimacy.
The precious things I have shared with her.
I know her quiet, love, and allure.
Her passion and fervent desires.
The length of attention she requires.
I know her lips when she kisses me.
Playing in her hair makes her sleepy.
I know her petals, like a flower,
and how many times she comes per hour.

Silver Light

Breezes from the window
share dances with your hair,
And robes upon the floor
leave both our bodies bare.
Silver light, moonbeams,
glisten on your skin.
Your gasps are soft and gentle.
You feel me from within.
Your thighs spread gently hither,
you're arching into me.
I feel your body quiver
and release in ecstasy.

<u>Bewitching</u>

After midnight,
the witching hour,
she casts her spell on me.

I lie in wait.
She will devour,
with hunger, 'til I'm free.

Evening Sky

I knew a woman once
with hair like the evening sky.
When she smiled at me,
she had a twinkle in her eye.
Her legs were long like towers;
she stood high over me.
And though she had long stature,
her face was clear to see.
She made her presence known,
like Venus in my own heart.
She gave her love with care
and swore we would never part.
Oh, but my sweet love is gone now,
never to look back.
And she has turned me into
the worst insomniac.
Sleep is hard to come by,
for the ebony of night
looks like my departed,
and I'm restless for the light.
Perhaps upon the breaking sun,
shining through the dawn,
I'll defeat the night
that holds me captive like a pawn.

The Right Words

I want the right words for you.
The right words to make you love me again.
The right words to remind you
of why you loved me before.
But I can't find the right words.
If I could put all my love in a glass bottle,
I would ask you to drink it,
and you would swell with love.
You would feel my love inside you,
and it would warm you.
It would remind you what it feels like to love me,
and you would love me again.
I want to hear your words
and why you don't love me anymore.
You can't just say you don't without a reason.
You loved me once before.
You loved me twice before.
Our love was broken,
but we put it back together again,
and it was ours.
Tell me you love me again.
Just say the right words.

These Quiet Arms

These are small, quiet arms wrapped around this body.
Alone, in the night and day, it's just me in here.
They speak to no one, tell no one of my secrets.
They do not reveal the truth in how they appear.

These are cold, quiet arms surrounding this body.
They are not here for my comfort, much as I try.
They pretend to be useful; deceiving, they are.
I hold myself tightly. I hold me and I cry.

Have these arms been cruel to someone else?
I consider my past transgressions.
I ask these arms what they have done
and if they have learned their lessons.

I have tried to walk the narrow path,
carefully toe the line.
But I've been left with these small, cold arms.
These quiet arms of mine.

A Reminder

Do you remember me beside you?
In front of you, behind you?
Do you remember me inside you?
Let these words remind you.

Ten Years

About a decade went by when
we were smoothing and roughing.
I thought I found forever,
and I wrote almost nothing.

Even with our ups and downs,
I didn't have much to say.
Not sure how to express it.
"I'm just fine again today?"

I cannot convey it now.
This boiling puddle of tears.
What we have been reduced to.
I wasted ten fucking years.

<u>Indelible</u>

We shared so many things
that are forevermore branded in my mind and heart.
I hesitated to open up to you,
but honestly you had me from the start.

We shared laughs and tears.
We cried. We danced even when you didn't want to.
We talked for hours.
I fell in love and gave everything to you.

The personal moments,
the intimacy we shared together,
marked me for life.
I thought we'd see forever.

Although we're strangers now,
you've been permanently etched in my memory.
I want to be just as indelible to you.
I don't want you to forget me.

Fossils

Blue crystalline drops do cascade,
and into lonely clear, they fade,
until the color drains away
from my tomorrow's yesterday.

It isn't what I thought I knew,
but what I know for me was true,
and even if the lie was real,
I could not fake what I can't feel.

The sorrow lingers dark and heavy.
Emotions gather to a bevy.
I've pushed away my moments passed.
Utterances I thought would last.

Carved in stone; etched into my soul.
How shamelessly you did cajole.
A fool at heart, I wish to hold
the warmth before the love runs cold.

Yet time will pass into the earth,
and sand and water give rebirth
to fossils' promise of the past.
Impressions. Things not meant to last.

<u>Layers</u>

You used to be so angry and aggressive.
It scared me but I was attracted to it.
I wanted to penetrate your exterior.
I wanted you to share your vulnerabilities with me.
You let me in. You showed me beneath your surface.
I watched your layers peel away.
I got to see your softness.

The Shower

I close my eyes
and wipe back streaming bubbles from my face.
The water closes over me.
I hurt for your embrace.

Your naked body close to mine,
I open up my eyes.
I look at you. You're staring back,
I quickly realize.

You have this look upon your face
while your eyes gaze at me.
I'm not secure in what it means,
although it's all I see.

It draws me in, I'm almost shy,
but feeling wanted too.
Our bodies touch. Our lips soon meet.
I'm so in love with you.

Black and Blue

Do you think that I don't know?
Perhaps I didn't hear?
You haven't exactly been
the boyfriend of the year.
I gave you what you wanted.
I fell in love with you.
Why did you try so damned hard
to leave me black and blue?

Last Night

Where was your man last night?
Was he holding you tight?

Was he alone with someone else? Are you even sure?
The truth, for you, is hard to find; it remains obscure.

What happened to the leash many other women have?
You didn't need one, right? You're the only one he has.

Hey, I was that way once.
Yeah, I was that way too.
And little did I know
that he was out with you.

So, guess what, girl? It's payback time.
Yes, little did you see,
your perfect man up late last night,
was in the dark with me.

Tell Her

Let me write
about last night,
so that I won't forget.

I guess that I
still wonder why,
but do I feel regret?

Tell her,
Jennifer,
that I said hello.
Tell her,
Jennifer,
you were good to go.

Feed her no line.
Say girl of mine,
now hold on really tight.

Listen here,
the truth is dear,
I was with April last night.

<u>Scribble</u>

Staring at a white rectangle,
trying to translate thoughts like a mage.
When I try to write about you,
I see lots of scribbles on the page.

I'll need some white-hot sorcery,
a firing wand; a magic stick,
to get me from point A to Z.
Gonna hit this paper with a trick.

I can't get my charming words out,
to free myself from this wordless hell.
You are robbing me of relief.
I will concoct a magical spell.

Give me back my voice. Let me out!
Jagged lines furiously askew.
I'm making my choice. Goodbye now.
I'm getting you out. I'm scribbling you.

I'm using a fine tip, for sure.
A mute brain. A waste. Meet a dead line.
No words, just this angry scrawling.
Stopping fast and silent, right on tine.

Now, do you see what I did there?
You're nothing more than scribbles to me.
I tear you off and ball you up.
Poof! You are long gone. Pure wizardry.

The Only Truth I See

I wonder if you see my empty, vague expressions.
I can practice your style
and give some false impressions.

My watchful eye follows your movements. I cry for you,
out of this desperate pain,
when there's nothing more to do.

I'm aware now that you wish I'd simply disappear,
so, you could worry less
and your conscience would be clear.

How could you turn on me? How could it mean so little?
How could I be fooled,
your sincerity so brittle?

Your feelings and your answers, you took them all, you know.
I admit, I'm broken.
I was sad to see them go.

I had to learn the hard way that you never loved me.
This truth is a tough lesson.
The only one I see.

I Remember the Room

Moonlight seeping through the curtains.
Two inhabiting the dark room.
Music grinding, continuing,
it surrounded us like a tomb.

Like everything had stopped, and we
were the only ones left alive.
Everything else ceased to exist
but our bodies; yours inside mine.

Inexplicable emotion,
riding nakedness as if one.
You were my god and my devil.
Your navel inked with tribal sun.

I still feel your hands on my skin,
your tongue searching between my thighs.
I reached ecstasy you gave me.
I don't need to apologize.

Rising, falling, bodies combined.
It felt something like love to me,
and bittersweet this longing is.
Something that can no longer be.

Embers

Our passion, our love, our burning desire,
now just a memory in a long-ended fire.

Inside of us blazed an omnipotent flame.
A condition I believed could never be tame.

Beyond understanding, it tried to transcend.
So ne'er did I think that it would once end.

Toward the last of our final days,
it showed itself in mysterious ways.

It seemed that our fire was dying out.
This is seldom what we were about.

Deep in my heart, no other's the same.
I cannot forget your beautiful name.

Now just memories that no one remembers,
in the end was nothing but embers.

<u>Stuck</u>

If I break free of these chains,
wherein would I find my gains?
I look beyond my here and now,
and I see only grey somehow.
As if reality will always be
this life I do not want for me.
If I am brave within this space,
Can I find my proper place?

Unshackled

You don't fucking own me.
I'm not your little toy.
I am not your servant.
A puppet you employ.

You don't dictate my life.
Not here to quench your thirst.
My health, not your plaything.
I will not put you first.

You destroyed the footings.
You drove everything out
with no concept of what
compassion is about.

Those years of toiling away
now mostly for your gain.
My hard work was futile.
My loyalty in vain.

Starting Over

I'm starting over at
the age of forty-five.
If I stay true to me,
I think that I'll survive.

<u>Found</u>

Deep blue, I've found you, hiding in the sky.
It's only now that you've appeared that I can answer why.
It's not until you find the bliss that brings you to a high,
that you can open up your hand and grab onto the sky.

Spring Morning

When morning breaks with sunlight,
and birds are up in song,
I almost wonder if the night
has lasted all too long.
Although my eyes are heavy,
I cannot rest my head.
I must wait up for lovely
morning air instead.
How brilliant is the morning
when shining through the trees.
How cooling is the window
when bringing in the breeze.
How perfect is the weather
at seventy-two degrees.
How much I do enjoy
every one of these.

<u>I Used To</u>

In nature, I looked for oracles around.
I used to think there were replies in its sound.

There has always been something about a tree
that captivates, bedazzles, and speaks to me.

Maybe holding answers. So mysterious.
So I kept waiting, endlessly curious.

But I didn't find responses I searched for,
so I do not question the trees anymore.

If not outside me, within perhaps instead,
answers may not be up, so I'll look ahead.

Transition

You're shedding weighted skin,
ridding that heavy shell.
Stripping barriers.
Becoming yourself.

They see someone different,
but you feel something else.
You're taking your lumps.
You're covered in welts.

Don't let them tear you down.
Don't listen or falter.
Do keep standing strong.
Define your altar.

Attempts to demean you,
whatever is dispelled,
cannot change the truth
of what is compelled.

Don't answer to others
for being who you are.
You can't surrender
when you've come so far.

Your face is familiar.
You've changed, yet you're the same.
I knew you before,
by another name.

Fitting transformation.
A metamorphosis.
Fierce awakening.
Righteous genesis.

About the Author

April Seymour

A self-published author of fiction and poetry, April strives to give her readers the same sense of immersion she experiences when reading a good book and enjoys exploring social and psychological themes. Native to upstate New York, she holds a Bachelor of Arts with a concentration in psychology and is a proud mother of one amazing daughter.

Books By This Author

Violin

Contemporary fiction
Psychological fiction

Stumbling hazily through
the days of her late
husband's funeral services,
Marla Mason's mourning
period is interrupted when
a moving truck appears
across the street. As she becomes acquainted with her
neighbor, Isaac Michaels, she finds his wife to be cold
and unfriendly and becomes increasingly wary of her.

Trying desperately to bury the skeletons in her closet,
newlywed, Fallon Michaels, moves to upstate New
York with her husband, only to find she can't run from
her sordid past. When Isaac connects with the woman
across the street, Marla, an older woman grieving the
loss of her husband and daughter, Fallon's behavior
becomes increasingly suspicious and avoidant, and a
web of secrets begins to unravel.

(Content guidance: sensitive subjects.)